NIFITSA

Eleni Philippou is a Greek-South African poet and academic based in the United Kingdom. Her award-winning poems have been published in a number of international magazines and anthologies, and have been translated into German and Polish.

© 2025, Eleni Philippou. All rights reserved. No part of this book may be reproduced, stored in a retrieval system, or transmitted in any form or by any means, whether electronic, mechanical, photocopying, recording, or otherwise, without the prior written permission of the publisher, except in the case of brief quotations used in reviews or scholarly works.

This work may not be used for text and data mining, including (without limitation) the training of artificial intelligence technologies or systems. The author and publisher expressly reserve all rights and opt out of any applicable text and data mining exceptions.

ISBN: 978-1-917617-52-9

Cover designed by Aaron Kent

Edited and Typeset by Aaron Kent

The author has asserted their right to be identified as the author of this Work in accordance with the Copyright, Designs and Patents Act 1988.

Broken Sleep Books Ltd
PO BOX 102
Llandysul
SA44 9BG

CONTENTS

ΕΚΚΙΝΗΣΗ / EKKINISI / START

PELION	11
SIMERA	13
NIFITSA	15
LOVER	16
WORLD'S EDGE	17
BLUE BELTON	18
THANATOS	19
KOLOKYTHA	20

ΑΝΑΧΩΡΗΣΗ / ANAHORISI / DEPARTURE

TACIT	23
WIZEN	25
NICHTOPOULI	26
HOROSCOPE	31
TRACT	32
IN ETERNAL	33

ΕΠΙΣΤΡΟΦΗ / EPISTROFI / RETURN

PARE	37
FATHER OF HISTORY	38
TOPOS	39
REMAIN	40
VICIOUS	41
CROSSINGS	43

GLOSSARY	45
ACKNOWLEDGEMENTS	47

Nifitsa

Eleni Philippou

Broken Sleep Books

Note: Renderings from Greek into English are largely phonetic transcriptions pronounceable to the English ear. Letters and digraphs pronounced as /i/ are transcribed as i. In instances of Greek place names, the most commonly used English version of the Greek name has been used.

Εκκίνηση
Ekkinisi
Start

PELION

The stone taverna

in the catted square.

The youngest couple.

She wears his jacket, smoking,

unspeaking. He eats

his sausage stew.

A day of orchards,

jade and cider red.

Mid-September frost.

She lets him desecrate her

so she would love him

like the ones before.

The sturdy root.

She calls as he enters.

The heart,

leaf-bound, apple-round

is so. Claimed.

Just barely.

After the organic fall,

a broken sleep. Through

the window

red apples like robins

weigh down trees.

Untarnished, gleam.

SIMERA

Elafonisos –

transparent the sea,

smothered in mottled starfish and black urchins.

I sit in my plastic tent, door flapping madly.

A northern wind beats back from the German nudists

who occupy the beach, penises hanging,

shrivelled crimson things.

I stare.

Each chalky pebble, round as a deficit nought.

"Cheap cheap," sing the birds. The cicadas hum,

"Not even your sea. Not even your sea."

*

In Attica,

from the hotel rooftop

I watch the erection of tents.

Your people carrying banners and rough signs.

They come in waves and wash the grey cement

with the paraffin grit of Molotovs.

They break upon the shoreline
of police shields,
the tainted words *drachmi* and *dollaria*.
evro.

					*

As you enter the ward you pay your *fakelaki* –
pearl-white casing for an ashen owl face –
and the doctor listens to the watery murmur in your chest,
and it beats and it beats,
but only because you paid to make it beat.

NIFITSA

In Modern Greek folklore a tale exists in which an unhappy bride is transformed into a weasel. In the past it was considered an ill omen for a weasel to be seen near households with a bride-to-be.

The vista from the Cretan dune –

a vast expanse of sea, cobalt upon cobalt,

building towards the horizon. Your figure now striding,

upright, pulling me forward with a primordial stealth.

Bent over from the hot wind

howling forth from Africa's northern shore,

lips blister-chapped and spine taut, I follow.

At the very bottom: a cave with the buried skull of a weasel,

just visible through the sand,

remembered from the year before

where we camped the night, and slept fitfully of our future.

That afternoon, as you enter me

slowly, tightening your arms around my shoulders, I think:

this is what it feels like, to be married,

to be in the infancy of love. And I love you

with all of me. And your release is the fullest thing, the total.

LOVER

On Loutro's sea edge

he cleaned

fish of tattered silver.

It came from the reef.

Knife-flick scaled-slick

and snapped it shut

in one crack bite.

Blood brutal.

He bludgeoned it once,

then twice,

with the knife's blunt handle.

Red in the

slow-waving weed.

It dimmed.

And with that death,

he flaunted

an instinct unbetrayed.

WORLD'S EDGE

Our love was like a canvas shelter,
provisional, dismantled
in the wake of winter.

At Seitan Limania, we
trekked down to the beach,
invisible from the cliff above.

We made camp at dusk,
cooked rice and beans,
sliced pomegranates,
picked out the pips,
told stories of the netherworld.
Your imagination
charged my desire,
made me want you always.

While you slept, just beyond
my hand's reach,
I got up to watch the blackened sea.
The rocks, vertical, near-human,
caught in the moment before life.

BLUE BELTON

Elounda, Elounda, Elounda,
that town on Crete's northern coast.
A name like a bird's call, like a tweet, and a-twitter,
a dog's gruff, a barking as you lift the scruff
of the neck. Like a hex, like a cough, like a hee-haw,
for every donkey in Greece, for the island of
olive and more.

That abandoned dog,
you called Haros, named for death,
sat, then sank, curled in
the crib of the car's deep floor.
Haros counted every flea, every sandfly
that fed off of his mottled coat, while the boats in the harbour
bobbed and rocked,
and we asked for the central *plateia*.

He cried through the night, shed his skin like a selkie,
became your furred brother. A scrawn, forlorn.

If I called you now, out of the blue, like Elounda's blue,
what would I say, and how could I come back again?
You had a mane of hair, like a lion. A deep grey shag.
Like an English setter we found on a beach.

THANATOS

He follows, obedient and soundless,

thin as death's scythe. We walk

on the broken

back of the pavement,

the drain, guttural, sucks in plastic bags

and brown water.

An older man asks us, matter-of-factly,

eyes glued on that wrecked dog, "What is he?".

Like asking a football score, the day of the week,

the bus schedule. And, the question barks,

trips over itself, "What is that bone, that snout?

Why bother?"

KOLOKYTHA

The strand's white pebbles
pick up the dusk light.
The pervasive grey seeps
like dye into the conversation,
and the dog limps, beat tired.

I want us to be still now, to cease
the constant churning, the tumbling sea.
Bow break and slow sift, tide in and through,
blue black and bream clean. The way to
the boats washes us out.

Αναχώρηση
Anahorisi
Departure

TACIT

In the dark

you became an animal:

gaunt, with fearful eyes.

Your beard, a goat's, and the heart,

a tiny sparrow in my hands.

Heightened pulse, core aflutter,

panic.

*

At school they told us, "Do you know that

to God, your life is worth more

than that of a common sparrow?"

You were worth more

than a sparrow to me.

More than God.

*

As a child I watched a hoopoe

in the garden and drew it

in burnt orange with a pluming crest.

I sketched fragile sea urchins,
images from nature.
Then I grew up and stopped drawing
but doodled small things for you:
a donkey, a dog.

*

To be without you now
is death, an olive wreath
drying out in the sun,
a stuffed bird in a cabinet.

*

When you wouldn't anymore,
I broke like an egg,
yolk for blood, shell for bone.

WIZEN

It's August that's the cruellest month,
with its summer fires,
its stony beach, its relentless heat.

*

I have a photo of you
standing on a cliff at Agios Pavlos,
sun-blasted back to me, looking outwards
towards the arid Libyan Coast.
The dog – scraggly, all-suffering –
in tow. Before the dust engulfed us,
stung our faces with serrated grains,
made us blind to the way ahead.

*

In the white-washed bedroom of that holiday let,
in the withering late afternoon, the confusion of wanting,
unwanting. The adrenalin-tremble of our limbs,
the pulling out, without warning,
a withdrawal from our life.

NICHTOPOULI

August

Night bird, night jar,

made of black down and gristle.

Will you turn into a church, a tree, a house

until you morph no more?

Nesting at Skaloma by the

sea of oil, of grey stone, of old shell.

We watch the clouds:

the way they build.

And the birds like bats

flit and swoop. A stirring wind.

Your eyes are blue, Margrete.

Do you see?

September

Fyssas, fyssas,

on the streets of Kypseli.

Do you blow out the dregs of history?

Unfeather the nest

woven of twine and bark?

"I don't know, Mimi," she says on the phone.

"I don't know," she repeats,

on the tram at Neos Kosmos.

I get off at the wrong stop.

October

When we first met

you took me to Exarcheia

where they shot him.

Dried out carnations and graffiti.

A tree with rose pomegranates.

We met your father in the street

outside his shop.

A hole in the wall,

concealed while they riot

and break up Athens.

He remembered Asimos rolling a wheel

down the street back in the 70s. "The madman," he laughed.

November

As a little boy you would roll oranges

into the road, under car wheels.

You started your own political party

with Pavlos and Magdalini.

The three of you, tiny and so serious,

put up hand drawn posters

on the streets of Brachami.

The neighbours still remember it.

December

I needed to suffer to see you.

It didn't sit, the words didn't catch, the soul didn't hear.
And the heart, it hardened and broke. I was dead to your story, to the acts and the snow and the cold of the old winter clock.

You told me that you didn't love me like you used to, and that you thought I didn't love you at all.

The country changed, we changed.

HOROSCOPE

You dreamt once that you wore a thick chain

with a golden crab medallion. In the dream, it meant a passing.

In a sequestered moment you fucked her and relaxed, slept.

"It meant nothing," you said, "it wasn't betrayal."

But it was death, side-walking into its vault of a shell.

TRACT

Bacteria bloom, like algae, in the urethra,

flourish in the fleshy enclaves of the kidneys.

A gradual rise of temperature,

blood speckling the urine,

the doctor explaining in her unmodulated voice

the mechanisms at play. Somehow,

even the microbes denounce us.

IN ETERNAL

My grief

for you bangs

like a door

in the night.

It opens and closes

with the erratic winds

of memory.

I have lost you,

I think.

Not in this house of the heart,

but out in the world

where nothing claims

your presence any longer.

The neutral smell

of the linen sheets;

the lamplight —

white as calcium;

the dog's bowl,

empty, clean.

Επιστροφή
Epistrofi
Return

PARE

To recede like a badger

into the loam and quiet.

To watch the weaver birds

pull the palm leaves into strips

and sew their structures

only to be unwoven by the

female's disapproving glance.

*

The elemental thing between us

snapped, like a brittle twig,

that night in the village when you

sat awake, active-tense

that I may touch you.

*

I want to whittle away every memory

of you but even splinters,

invisible to the eye,

touch a nerve.

FATHER OF HISTORY

It began with one reference to Herodotus –

the unbalancing of nature, the decimation

of the ancient forests – and through that

I thought to love you, to make you, Him.

But those elevated words dwindled into

questions about dinner, routines, hair removal.

The boredom crept in discreetly, like a cat

slipping in through the bedroom window,

a headless mouse in its jaws.

TOPOS

The map – threadbare, a parchment piece –
       navigated us over turnstiles and kissing gates,
through black-faced sheep, wooden fences.
       You read the Oxford field, its ridges and furrows,
with a historian's eye: the story of medieval
       labour banding together to till the ground, ploughing
until the flat became an undulating wave.
       Our legs ached. We settled like birds
on driftwood, and spoke of our barren future.
       Now you are a furrow too: our winter walks
pressing into the earth of my memories.

REMAIN

Here, among the criss-cross of

dead branches. A decade

of knocking about in gusty halls,

black gowns, clinking knives and forks.

Sipping tea before supper

in idle chat. Relations diminishing

like the December sun. My resolve,

a tender leaf, claimed by the

cold, plucked by the

chapped hands of winter.

VICIOUS

I can feign love: the posture,
the morning caresses, the interlocked walk
down Woodstock Road when it's cold.
It wasn't always so.

*

You were the resurrection of feeling.
Pole raising, flag bearing.

And you said, "There is no direct line
from antiquity to us," as we walked
through a gorge in central Crete.
But I read Hellenistic images into you:
geometric patterns on ancient vases,
red waistcoats, embroidered doilies,
the stickiness of preserved fig.

In this heart of Greece,
a branch swept us into the sun, into
chirruping August. There we recoiled,
grew burnt, hard like day-old bread.

Perhaps you couldn't bear the close scrutiny
of epsilon, olive, and Ypsilantis,
the accusative case.
We became a folktale,
where I tell the story of you, of us, always.

*

Do you wake in the pit of Heraklion's morning
wishing you weren't around,
or that I was around, that the world
was less hostile and you could reach out your arm
to find me curled up on the edge of the bed?

Now that I have loved you,
nothing is near the same.

CROSSINGS

For more than a year after

I woke up every morning

miming the curve of our bodies,

throbbing with longing

in every cavity.

You said that even if I achieved nothing else with you,

I had made you a person. The words were,

"έχεις καταφέρει να με κάνεις άνθρωπο."

But I was made in your hands,

a wooden totem, a uterine gourd,

suddenly animated.

Now, I cross over into new arms, uninitiated hearts.

I perform the hand clasping, the cooking,

the lying in bed, watching TV, sleeping in,

and pressing the alarm.

Everyday. Yet.

GLOSSARY

Anahorisi	Αναχώρηση	Departure
Asimos	Άσιμος	Composer and Singer
Haros	Χάρος	Death/The Grim Reaper
Dollaria	Δολάρια	Dollars
Drachmi	Δραχμή	Drachma
Ekkinisi	Εκκίνηση	Start
Epistrofi	Επιστροφή	Return
Evro	Ευρώ	Euro
Fakelaki	Φακελάκι	Small Envelope/Bribe
Fyssas	Φύσσας	Anti-fascist rapper killed by Golden Dawn in 2013. Also play on φυσάς (fysas) "to blow"
Nichtopouli	Νυχτοπούλι	Night bird
Nifitsa	Νυφίτσα	Weasel
Plateia	Πλατεία	Town square
Simera	Σήμερα	Today
Thanatos	Θάνατος	Death
Topos	Τόπος	Place
Ypsilantis	Υψηλάντης	Revolutionary in the Greek War of Independence

ACKNOWLEDGEMENTS

Poems included in this pamphlet have been published in the following magazines and anthologies:

"Pelion" in *The Apple Anthology* (Nine Arches Press)

"Simera" in *The Mays Anthology* (Varsity Publications), republished with *Futures: Poetry of the Greek Crisis* (Penned in the Margins), and *Tripwire 14: The Red Issue*. Translated into Polish for Festiwal Prapremier 2016.

"Lover" in *The Materialist*

"Thanatos" and "Topos" in *Migration and Society*

"Tacit" in *Ambit*

"Nichtopouli" in *Futures: Poetry of the Greek Crisis* (Penned in the Margins). Translated into German and republished with *Kleine Tiere zum Schlachten: Neue Gedichte aus Griechenland* (parasitenpresse).

"Horoscope" and "Pare" in *Oxford Poetry*

"In Eternal" in *New Contrast–South African Literary Journal*

LAY OUT YOUR UNREST

www.ingramcontent.com/pod-product-compliance
Lightning Source LLC
LaVergne TN
LVHW041310080426
835510LV00009B/946